Syria and The Enemy

Free Aleppo University

Play

Syria and The Enemy

Copyright 2017© by Free Aleppo University

ISBN 10: 1545072256

ISBN 13: 978-1545072257

Dedication…

We dedicate this book to the martyrs of the Great Syrian Revolution.. to those who sacrificed the most important thing they have for the best of Syria.. for the best of our children.. for the best of our future.. for them, we dedicate this work.

This publication is owned by the Free Aleppo University. Nobody has the right to ask for its ownership except for the administration of the Free University of Aleppo in addition to the members of the team who performed the work.

Acknowledgment

As a supervisor for this work, I was really surprised for the idea of hardworking girls who decided to do something magnificent. These girls were planning to make a surprise and they wanted to hide it from me and when I insisted to get the idea of their work, I was really enthusiastic when they told me that they are preforming a play. I thought that they are laughing but when they disclose the manuscript of their play, I was sure that in front of the eyes of mine, there is a group of girls who can do whatever they want.. a group of girls who own a dream to make a change in this life. Each girl in this group own her own special dreams but together, they make a wish and worked hard to make it true. I am really thankful for all your efforts and for all the great work you have done. Hereby is a list of those strong and dreamy girls who were the real authors of this lovely idea, this lovely play and this nice and great project.

- Alaa Karry
- Noor AL-Ali
- Hiba Dela'a
- Fatema Sadek
- Fatima AL-zahraa Satoof
- Bushra Al- Abdallah
- Hindea Halima
- Rama Haj Mohammed
- Ekhlas Osman
- Israa Saleeby
- Bayan Al shab
- Amenah kokash
- Huda Fakeeh

No words can describe who thankful I am for you.. for your idea and for all the time you spent practicing and performing rehearsals for this play.
Now, after you know how lovely your work, you can have other ideas and

other plans and other projects to perform. Trust yourselves because I trust you.. you can do your dreams and you can achieve your goals.
I really acknowledge what have you done.

Mustafa Kayyali

Type of the work : paly

Full title : Syria and the Enemy

Authors : Free Aleppo University with a cast consists of : Alaa Karry, Noor AL-Ali, Hiba Dela'a, Fatima AL-zahraa Satoof, Bushra Al- Abdallah, Hindea Halima, Rama Haj Mohammed, Ekhlas Osman, Israa Saleeby, Bayan Al shab, Amenah kokash, Huda Fakeeh.

Type of work : Play

Genre : Tragedy

Language : English

Time and place written : In Idleb, Syria. March, 2017

Date of first publication : Apr, 2017

Publisher : Mustafa Kayyali

Tone : the authors of this play focuses upon the situation of war in Syria and how is that they enemy of Syria caused a great destruction for the country.

Setting (time) : In 2017. The play talk about the effects of the Syrian war since 2011 till nowadays.

Setting (place) : Idleb, Syria.

Protagonist : Syria and its cities

Major conflict : Syria and its cities who were having a lovely and nice life as the first part and the enemy of Syria who wanted to cause great destruction for the country and its cities.

Rising action : The enemy is trying to destroy Syria and its cities.

Climax : When the enemy started to destroy the Syrian cities, one by one.

Falling action : the moment when the Syrian cities united against the enemy and caused him a great loss.

Themes : The heroism and love; the danger of isolation against the Syrian cities.

Symbols : cries, laughs.

foreshadowing : the talk of the Enemy for the Syrian cities and how he tried to overcome them and how they united together and defeated him.

Writer of the text (Rama)

Today I will tell you about a story This story is different than other stories. I am going to talk about Syria the mother, the compassionate and the affectionate. It is our hometown..

Syria is a strange mystery. It's long history is full of events.. It is famous for its generosity. People, cities and all villages.. they all generous for others. Syria own wealth and ruins. During history, Syria faced various types of hostility and injustice. Now, I am leaving Syria to tell you about her self

Syria (Noor):

I am Syria the glorious Syria , I am the strength ,I am mother of hope and I am the woman whose people are sad. Whose people are feeling with pain..

The enemy(Ekhlas):

Do you think you are strong ??!
you do not have any importance?
you have no
meaning , no history , nothing at
all.

Syria (Noor):

You are wrong O bad enemy! You
are very wrong! My history is full
of events and great works. My
people in the past made the
greatest victories , here is my
history to talk about me.

History (Hoda):

I am the history of Syria , I am it is so long history that extended through thousands of years since the beginning of alphabet , in my walls and temples, I contain the name of governors and successors.. some of them were bad while others were good ,I wrote it's battles and its conflicts and I know those who exploited since the date of crusaders till the occupation of

French forces till the war that occurs nowadays.

The enemy (Ekhlas):

Is this everything ?! give me one evidence to believe you.

Syria (Noor):

The largest evidence is my ruins ,I leave it to talk about me .

The ruins (Hiba):

I am ruins of Syria ,I am full of stories ,I tell a long time with each and every part of me. Each part of me has a story like the story of (Ras shamra) where there we found the first Alphabet in the history of humankind ,and many great castles like (Aleppo citadel,

Damascus citadel ,and listed Palmyra which was a great treasure loved and adored by.

The enemy: (Ekhlas):

You are a divided country and I will destroy you more than this Even the names of you cities are unknown.

Syria :

Shut up! My cites are the coolest cities in the world ,and they are the most beautiful places to visit.

Cities (Israa):

I am the cities of Syria .... In every part of me, there is beauty. In each part of me, you can see history.. like Damascus umayyads... ALepo Hamadanins .... Homs Khaled bin Alwaled and Daraa revolution.

Oh enemy , I have chosen three of my cities to tell about themselves.

Aleppo (Bayan) :

I am Aleppo , I am the height and greatness.. My houses fall down on heads of my people I am the city who have beautiful ruins and great places, I am Aleppo who belongs far away in the history. I am the protector of the North.. I am the treasure of Syria.

Idleb (Amenah):

I am Idleb I have the height and strength . I am the free Idleb. I am always wearing green all the year and my trees are always green. I am the house of history and container of treasures.. I am mother of love and generosity , I am essence of Syria.

Damascus (Alaa):

I am the Damascene jasmine ,I am the mother of civilization, I am the oldest city in the world.
I am the world of beauty , I am the paradise of the earth , I am the oldest capital in the world , I am the daughter of poets and

fiancé of novelists , I am the first and no one before me.

The enemy:

Let your useless and silly cities away from me. Let me tell you that you are the poorest country in the world and the most miserable cities in the world.

Syria :

Let me tell you something I have wealth and strength if you are face it, it will overwhelm you , I thank ALLAH for all these blesses.

The wealth (Boshra):

Will I know you about myself , I am the oil and gas , I'm the wheat and Cotton. I am fruits and vegetables, I am the great rivers of Syria , I am the great ground of AL –Sham's blessed land. I am the greatest nation in the world. You are stupid to talk about Syria. You are so weak and so bad enemy!

The enemy:

Me! Hhhhh... you still the poorest ,, your people are selfish and barbaric , stupid and exploited.

Syria (Noor):

he he he !! you tell a lie and you believe it !! my people are real, lovely and ideal. Here is my people who would like to talk about itself.

O people, speak now

The people (fatema):

I am the people of Syria , I have a big history and great civilization. I give it my life and for the sake of this civilization, I have spelt my blood. We will do everything to save Syria and keep it away from all disasters. We spent our blood and we are ready to do that again and again and again. It was one part and we will keep it one part. We will stay with our Syria forever. You have no place O bad enemy in our land.

The enemy :

Me! Dear Syria ,,

Do you know that true??

Your land is useless and dry ,
nothing is planted in your
lands?!!

(Syria) :

Enemy !! Do you know ??

You are ratty and petty ,, my
ground is the most blessed land
,and here is my ground to talk
about me ...

The ground (Fatema.S):

I'm the ground of Syria the blessed land by God, holy, protected and guaranteed by God. I'm the land that was decorated with the blood of the heroes , I'm the crossroad of civilizations and peoples. I'm the land of generosity that greeted it's guests with all generous.

(Syria):

Enough bad enemy, we stand up to gather and kill you and you will die alone!

(The enemy):

Me I'm absolutely the winner , and I will divide you and remove the ground and humanity.

(Syria):

Go away evil one! My pillars will remain steadfast you will never remove them I 'm the bride of world. God protects me from your aggression .. take your soldiers and leave ⬚

(Every one)

Syria we will stay with you forever and we can do it .

This publication is owned by the Free Aleppo University. Nobody has the right to ask for its ownership except for the administration of the Free University of Aleppo in addition to the members of the team who performed the work.

One again, I really would like to thank you, for making this work real. For all your hardworking for all the time and efforts you have spent.

- Alaa Karry
- Noor AL-Ali
- Hiba Dela'a
- Fatima AL-zahraa Satoof
- Bushra Al- Abdallah
- Hindea Halima
- Rama Haj Mohammed
- Ekhlas Osman
- Israa Saleeby
- Bayan Al shab
- Amenah kokash
- Huda Fakeeh
- Fatema Sadek

Wish you all the best and good luck for ever and ever and ever.

Mustafa Kayyali